MARK·TWAIN

a cat-tale

MARK · TWAIN

a cat-tale

Illustrated by
CHARLES BLACKMAN

My little girls — Susy, aged eight,
and Clara, six — often require me to
help them go to sleep, nights, by
telling them original tales. They
think my tales are better than
paregoric, and quicker. While I
talk, they make comments and ask
questions, and we have a pretty good
time. I thought maybe other little
people might like to try one of my
narcotics — so I offer this one.

National Library of Australia
Cataloguing-in-Publication data

Twain, Mark, 1835-1910.
    A cat-tale.

    ISBN 0 9587845 0 7

    1. Cats — Juvenile fiction. I. Blackman, Charles,
    1982-   . II. Title.

813'.4

Illustrations © 1987 by Charles Blackman

Produced by P.I.C. Pty Ltd
Box 4939, GPO Sydney, Australia 2001

First published in Australia by Ashton Scholastic Pty Limited 1987.

Printed in Hong Kong

NCE THERE WAS A noble big cat, whose Christian name was Catasauqua — because she lived in that region — but she did not have any surname, because she was a short-tailed cat — being a Manx — and did not need one. It is very just and becoming in a long-tailed cat to have a surname, but it would very ostentatious, and even dishonorable, in a Manx. Well, Catasauqua had a beautiful family of catlings; and they were of different colors, to harmonize with

ostentatious

CATASAUQUA

For the meanings of the words in color, turn to page 42 where 'Mr Webster' explains.

their characters. Cattaraugus, the eldest, was white and he had
high impulses and a pure heart; Catiline, the youngest, was black,
and he had a self-seeking nature, his motives were nearly always
base, he was truculent and insincere. He was vain and foolish,
and often said he would rather be what he was, and live like a
bandit, yet have none above him, than be a cat-'o-nine-tails and
eat with the King. He hated his harmless and unoffending little
catercousins, and frequently drove them from his presence with
imprecations, and at times even resorted to violence.

truculent

catercousins
imprecations

For the meanings
of the words
in color, turn
to page 42 where
'Mr Webster' explains.

...PAPA?

SUSY: What are catercousins, Papa?

Quarter-cousins — it is so set down in the big dictionary. You observe I refer to it every now and then. This is because I do not wish to make any mistakes, my purpose being to instruct as well as entertain. Whenever I use a word which you do not understand, speak up and I will look and find out what it means. But do not interrupt me except for cause, for I am always excited when I am erecting history, and want to get on. Well, one day Catasauqua met with a misfortune; her house burned down. It was the very day after it had been insured for double its value, too — how singular! Yes, and how lucky! This often happens. It teaches us that mere loading a house down with insurance isn't going to save it. Very well, Catasauqua took the insurance money

For the meanings of the words in color, turn to page 42 where 'Mr Webster' explains.

and built a new house; and a much better one, too; and what is more, she had money left to add a gaudy concatenation of extra improvements with. Oh, I tell you! What she didn't know about catallactics no other cat need ever try to acquire.

concatenations

catallactics

CLARA: What is catallactics, Papa?

The dictionary intimates in a nebulous way, that it is a sort of demi-synonym for the science commonly called political economy.

nebulous

demi-synonym

CLARA: Thank you, Papa.

Yes, behind the house she constructed a splendid large catadrome, and enclosed it with a caterwaul about nine feet high, and in the centre was a spacious grass plot where —

catadrome

caterwaul

CLARA: What is a catadrome, Papa?

I will look. Ah, it is a race course; I thought it was a ten-pin alley. But no matter; in fact, it is all the better; for cats do not play ten-pins, when they are feeling well, but they *do* run races, you know; and the spacious grass plot was for cat fights, and other free exhibitions; and for ball games — three-cornered cat, and all that sort of thing; a lovely spot, lovely. Yes, indeed; it had a hedge of dainty little catkins around it, and right in the centre was a splendid great categorematic in full leaf, and —

catkins
categorematic

SUSY: What is a categorematic, Papa?

I think it's a kind of a shade tree, but I'll look. No — I was mistaken; it is a word: 'a word which is capable of being employed by itself as a term'.

SUSY: Thank you, Papa.

Don't mention it. Yes, you see, it wasn't a shade tree; the good Catasauqua didn't know that, else she wouldn't have planted it right there in the way; you can't run over a word like that, you know, and not cripple yourself more or less. Now don't forget that definition, it may come in handy to you some day — there is no telling — life is full of vicissitudes. Always remember, a categorematic is a word which a cat can use by herself as a term; but she mustn't try to use it along with another cat, for that is not the idea. Far from it. We have authority for it, you see — Mr. Webster; and he is dead, too, besides. It would be a noble good thing if his dictionary was, too. But that is too much to expect. Yes; well, Catasauqua filled her house with internal improvements — catcalls in every room, and they are Oh, ever so much handier

vicissitudes

cat-call

For the meanings of the words in color, turn to page 42 where 'Mr Webster' explains.

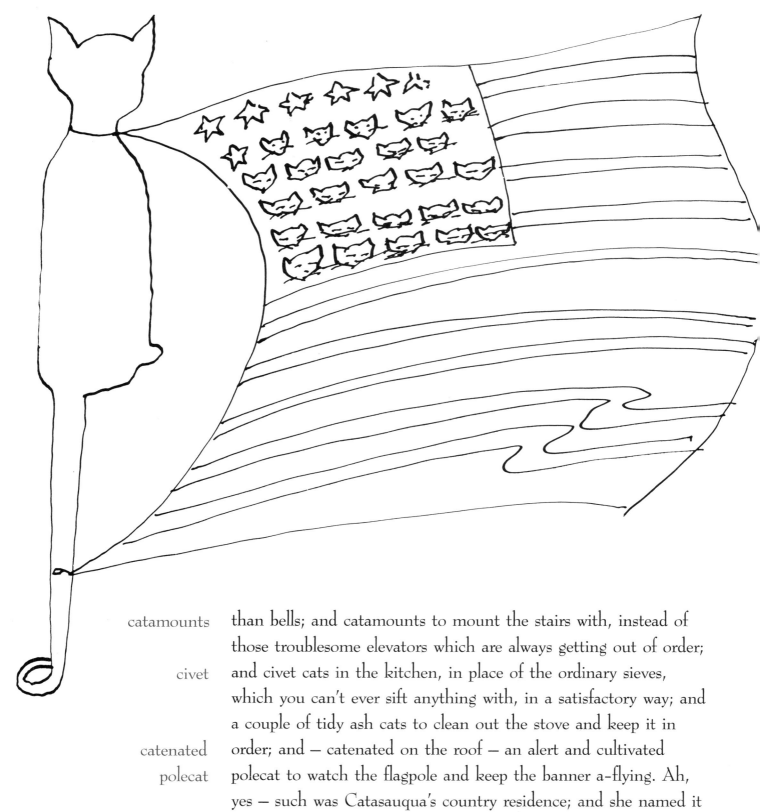

catamounts   than bells; and catamounts to mount the stairs with, instead of
             those troublesome elevators which are always getting out of order;
civet   and civet cats in the kitchen, in place of the ordinary sieves,
             which you can't ever sift anything with, in a satisfactory way; and
             a couple of tidy ash cats to clean out the stove and keep it in
catenated   order; and — catenated on the roof — an alert and cultivated
polecat   polecat to watch the flagpole and keep the banner a-flying. Ah,
             yes — such was Catasauqua's country residence; and she named it
             Kamscatka — after her dear native land far away.

sevenFor the meanings
of the words
in color, turn
to page 42 where
'Mr Webster' explains.

CLARA: What is catenated, Papa?

Chained, my child. The polecat was attached by a chain to some
object upon the roof contiguous to the flagpole. This was to
retain him in his position.

contiguous

CLARA: Thank you, Papa.

The front garden was a spectacle of sublime and bewildering
magnificence. A stately row of flowering catalpas stretched from
the front door clear to the gate, wreathed from stem to stern

sublime

catalpas

tendrils
congeries
catapetalous

with the delicate tendrils and shining scales of the cat's-foot ivy, whilst ever and anon the enchanted eye wandered from congeries of lordly cattails and kindred catapetalous blooms too deep for utterance, only to encounter the still more entrancing vision of catnip without number and without price, and swoon away in ecstasy unutterable, under the blissful intoxication of its too, too fragrant breath!

BOTH CHILDREN: Oh, how lovely!

You may well say it. Few there be that shall look upon the like again. Yet was not this all; for hither to the north boiled the majestic cataract in unimaginable grandiloquence and thither to the south sparkled the gentle catadupe in serene and incandescent tranquillity, whilst far and near the halcyon brooklet flowed between!

cataract
grandiloquence
catadupe
incandescent
halcyon

CATULLUS

For the meanings of the words in color, turn to page 42 where 'Mr Webster' explains.

BOTH CHILDREN: Oh, how sweet! What is a catadupe, Papa?
Small waterfall, my darlings. Such is Webster's belief. All things
being in readiness for the housewarming, the widow sent out her
invitations, and then proceeded with her usual avocations. For   avocations
Catasauqua was a widow — sorrow cometh to us all. The
husband-cat — Catullus was his name — was no more. He was of
a lofty character, brave to rashness, and almost incredibly
unselfish. He gave eight of his lives for his country, reserving only
one for himself. Yes, the banquet having been ordered, the good
Catasauqua tuned up for the customary morning-song,
accompanying herself on the catarrh, and her little ones joined in.   catarrh

These were the words:

There was a little cat,
And she caught a little rat,
Which she dutifully rendered to her mother,
Who said 'Bake him in a pie,
For his flavor's rather high —
Or confer him on the poor, if you'd druther'.

Catasauqua sang soprano, Catiline sang tenor, Cattaraugus sang bass. It was exquisite melody; it would make your hair stand right up.

SUSY: Why, Papa, I didn't know cats could sing.

Oh, can't they, though! Well, these could. Cats are packed full of music — just as full as they can hold; and when they die, people remove it from them and sell it to the fiddle-makers. Oh, yes indeed. Such is Life.

SUSY: Oh, here is a picture! Is it a picture of the music, Papa?

Only the eye of prejudice could doubt it, my child.

prejudice

SUSY: Did you draw it, Papa?

I am indeed the author of it.

SUSY: How wonderful! What is a picture like this called, Papa?

A work of art, my child. There — do not hold it so close; prop it up on the chair, *three steps away*; now then — that is right; you see how much better and stronger the expression is than when it is close by. It is because some of this picture is drawn in perspective.

For the meanings of the words in color, turn to page 42 where 'Mr Webster' explains.

CLARA: Did you always know how to draw, Papa?

Yes. I was born so. But of course I could not draw at first as well as I can now. These things require study and practice. Mere talent is not sufficient. It takes a person a long time to get so he can draw a picture like this.

CLARA: How long did it take you, Papa?

Many years — thirty years, I reckon. Off and on — for I did not devote myself exclusively to art. Still, I have had a great deal of practice. Ah, practice is the great thing! It accomplishes wonders. Before I was twenty-five, I had got so I could draw a cork as well as anybody that ever was. And many a time I have drawn a blank in a lottery. Once I drew a check that wouldn't go; and after the war I tried to draw a pension, but this was too ambitious. However, the most gifted must fail sometimes. Do you observe those things that are sticking up, in this picture? They are not bones, they are paws; it is very hard to express the difference between bones and paws, in a picture.

SUSY: Which is Cattaraugus, Papa?

The little pale one that almost has the end of his mother's tail in his mouth.

SUSY: But, Papa, that tail is not right. You know Catasauqua was a Manx, and had a short one.

It is a just remark, my child; but a long tail was necessary, here, to express a certain passion, the passion of joy. Therefore the insertion of a long tail is permissible; it is called a poetic license. You cannot express the passion of joy with a short tail. Nor even extraordinary excitement. You notice that Cattaraugus is brilliantly excited; now nearly all of that verve, spirit, *élan*, is owing to his tail; yet if I had been false to art to be true to Nature, you would see there nothing but a poor little stiff and emotionless stump on that cat that would have cast a coldness

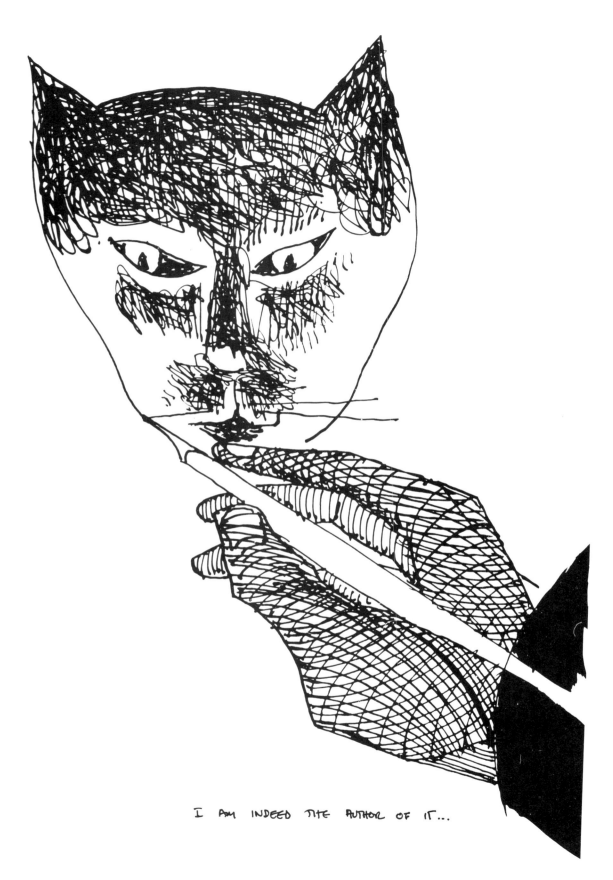

I AM INDEED THE AUTHOR OF IT...

VERVE. SPIRIT

over the whole scene; yet Cattaraugus was a Manx, like his mother, and had hardly any more tail than a rabbit. Yes, in art, the office of the tail is to express feeling; so, if you wish to portray a cat in repose, you will always succeed better by leaving out the tail. Now here is a striking illustration of the very truth which I am trying to impress upon you. I proposed to draw a cat recumbent and in repose; but just as I had finished the front end of her, she got up and began to gaze passionately at a bird and wriggle her tail in a most expressively wistful way. I had to finish her with that end standing, and the other end lying. It greatly injures the picture. For, you see, it confuses two passions together — the passion of standing up, and the passion of lying down.

recumbent

...THAN A RABBIT

For the meanings of the words in color, turn to page 42 where 'Mr Webster' explains.

These are incompatible; and they convey a bad effect to the picture by rendering it unrestful to the eye. In my opinion a cat in a picture ought to be doing one thing or the other; lying down or standing up, but not both. I ought to have laid this one down again, and put a brick or something on her; but I did not think of it at the time. Let us now separate these conflicting passions in this cat, so that you can see each by itself, and the more easily study it. Lay your hands on the picture, to where I have made those dots, and cover the rear half of it from sight — now you observe how reposeful the front end is. Very well; now lay your hand on the front end and cover *it* from sight — do you observe the eager wriggle in that tail? It is a wriggle which only the presence of a bird can inspire.

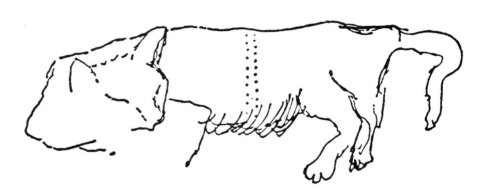

SUSY: You must know a wonderful deal, Papa.

I have that reputation — in Europe; but here the best minds superficial   think I am superficial. However, I am content; I make no defense; my pictures show what I am.

SUSY: Papa, I should think you would take pupils.

No, I have no desire for riches. Honest poverty and a conscience

torpid through virtuous inaction are more to me than corner lots  torpid
and praise.

    But to resume. The morning-song being over, Catasauqua told
Catiline and Cattaraugus to fetch their little books, and she
would teach them how to spell.

For the meanings
of the words
in color, turn
to page 42 where
'Mr Webster' explains.

BOTH CHILDREN: Why, Papa! Do cats have books?

catechisms   Yes, catechisms. Just so. Facts are stubborn things. After lesson,
              Catasauqua gave Catiline and Cattaraugus some rushes, so that
cat's cradle they could earn a little circus-money by building cat's cradles, and
              at the same time amuse themselves and not miss her; then she
              went to the kitchen and dining room to inspect the preparations
              for the banquet.

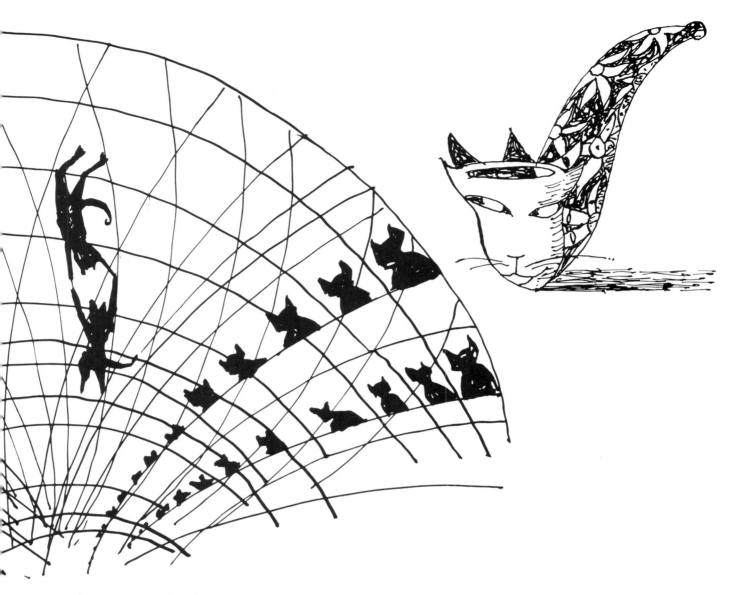

The moment her back was turned, Catiline put down his work and got out his catpipe for a smoke.

SUSY: Why, how naughty!

Thou has well spoken. It was disobedience; and disobedience is the flagship of the fleet of sin. The gentle Cattaraugus sighed and said: 'For shame, Catiline! How often has our dear mother told you not to do that! Ah, how can you thus disregard the commandments of the author of your being?'

SUSY: Why, what beautiful language, for such a little thing, *wasn't* it, Papa?

For the meanings of the words in color, turn to page 42 where 'Mr Webster' explains.

Rollo's mother
'Franconia series'
————
Popular children's
books written by
Jacob Abbott, who
lived from 1803 to
1879. There were
28 books about Rollo,
a boy who lived on a
New England farm;
the first was published
in 1834 or 1835.

'S'CAT!'

microscopic

Ah, yes, indeed. That was the kind of cat he was — cultivated,
you see. He had sat at the feet of Rollo's mother; and in the able
'Franconia Series' he had not failed to observe how harmoniously
gigantic language and a microscopic topic go together. Catiline
heard his brother through, and then replied with the
contemptuous ejaculation: 'S'scat!'

'ALAS...'

It means the same that Shakespeare means when he says, 'Go to'. Nevertheless, Catiline's conscience was not at rest. He murmured something about Where was the harm, since his mother would never know? But Cattaraugus said, sweetly but sadly, 'Alas, if we but do the right under restraint of authoritative observance, where then is the merit?'

For the meanings of the words in color, turn to page 42 where 'Mr Webster' explains.

SUSY: How *good* he was!

Monumentally so. The more we contemplate his character, the more sublime it appears. But Catiline, who was coarse and worldly, hated all lofty sentiments, and especially such as were stated in choice and lofty terms; he wished to resent this one, yet compelled himself to hold his peace; but when Cattaraugus said it over again, partly to enjoy the sound of it, but mainly for his brother's good, Catiline lost his patience, and said, 'Oh, take a walk!'

'OH, TAKE A WALK!'

Yet he still felt badly; for he knew he was doing wrong. He began to pretend he did not know it was against the rule to smoke his catpipe; but Cattaraugus, without an utterance, lifted an accusing paw toward the wall, where, among the illuminated mottoes hung this one:

mottoes

NO SMOKING. STRICTLY PROHIBITED.

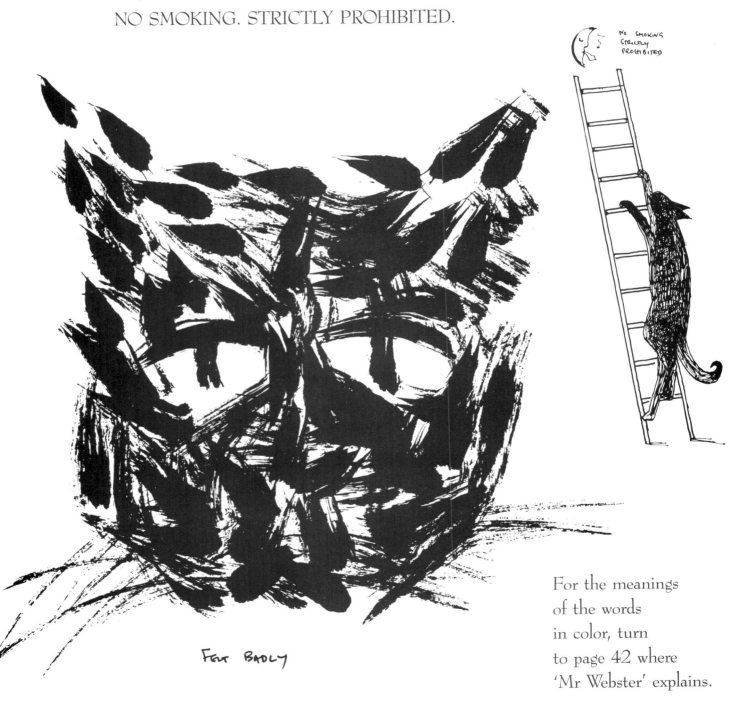

FELT BADLY

For the meanings
of the words
in color, turn
to page 42 where
'Mr Webster' explains.

TURNED PALE

Catiline turned pale; and, murmuring in a broken voice, 'I am undone — forgive me, Brother,' laid the fatal catpipe aside and burst into tears.

CLARA: Poor thing! It was cruel, *wasn't* it, Papa?

SUSY: Well but he oughtn't to done so, in the first place. Cattaraugus wasn't to blame.

CLARA: Why *Susy!* If Catiline didn't *know* he wasn't allowed —

SUSY: Catiline did know it — Cattaraugus told him so; and besides, Catiline —

CLARA: Cattaraugus only told Catiline that if —

'WHY, SUSY!'

SUSY: Why, *Clara!* Catiline didn't *need* for Cattaraugus to say
one single —

Oh, hold on! It's all a mistake! Come to look in the dictionary,
we are proceeding from false premises. The Unabridged says a
catpipe is 'a squeaking instrument used in play-houses to
condemn plays'. So you see it wasn't a pipe to smoke, after all;
Catiline *couldn't* smoke it; therefore it follows that he was simply
pretending to smoke it, to stir up his brother, that's all.

SUSY: But, Papa, Catiline might as well smoke as stir up his
brother.

CLARA: Susy, you don't like Catiline, and so whatever he does, it don't suit you, it ain't right; and he is only a little fellow, anyway.

SUSY: I don't *approve* of Catiline, but I *like* him well enough; I only say —

CLARA: What is approve?

SUSY: Why it's as if you did something, and I said it was all right. So *I* think he might as well smoke as stir up his brother. Isn't it so, Papa?

For the meanings of the words in color, turn to page 42 where 'Mr Webster' explains.

Looked at from a strictly mathematical point of view, I don't know, but it *is* a case of six-in-one-and-half-a-dozen-in-the-other. Still, *our* business is mainly with the historical facts; if we only get *them* right, we can leave posterity to take care of the moral aspects of the matter. To resume the thread of the narrative, when Cattaraugus saw that Catiline had not been smoking at all, but had only been making believe, and this too with the avowed object of fraternal aggravation, he was deeply hurt; and by his heat was beguiled into recourse to that bitter

posterity

fraternal

aggravation

beguiled

recourse

DEEPLY HURT

weapon, sarcasm; saying, 'The Roman Catiline would have betrayed his foe; it was left to the Catasauquian to refine upon the model and betray his friend.'

erudite
derisively
catachrestic

'Oh, a gaudy speech! — and very erudite and swell!' retorted Catiline, derisively, 'But just a *little* catachrestic'.

SUSY: What is catachrestic, Papa?

'Farfetched', the dictionary says. The remark stung Cattaraugus to the quick, and he called Catiline a catapult; this infuriated Catiline beyond endurance, and he threw down the gauntlet and called Cattaraugus a catso. No cat will stand that; so at it they

... A CATAPULT

SARCASM

For the meanings
of the words
in color, turn
to page 42 where
'Mr Webster' explains.

went. They spat and clawed and fought until they dimmed away and finally disappeared in a flying fog of cat fur.

CLARA: What is a catso, Papa?

'A base fellow, a rogue, a cheat,' says the dictionary. When the weather cleared, Cattaraugus, ever ready to acknowledge a fault, whether committed by himself or another, said, 'I was wrong, brother — forgive me. A cat may err — to err is cattish; but toward even a foreigner, even a wildcat, a catacaustic remark is in ill taste; how much more so, then, when a brother is the target!

catacaustic

Yes, Catiline, I was wrong; I deeply regret the circumstances. Here is my hand — let us forget the dark o'er-clouded past in the bright welkin of the present, consecrating ourselves anew to its nobler lessons, and sacrificing ourselves yet again, and forever if need be, to the thrice-armed beacon that binds them in one!'

SUSY: He was a splendid talker, *wasn't* he, Papa? Papa, what is catacaustic?

welkin

consecrating

thrice

Well, a catacaustic remark is a bitter, malicious remark — a sort
of — sort of — or a kind of a — well, let's look in the dictionary;
that is cheaper. Oh, yes, here it is: 'CATACAUSTIC, *n*; a caustic
curve formed by reflection of light.' Oh, yes, that's it.

SUSY: Well, Papa, what does *that* mean?

BRIGHT
WELKIN

For the meanings
of the words
in color, turn
to page 42 where
'Mr Webster' explains.

Mr Webster Explains...

Mr Noah Webster lived from 1758 to 1843. He began his career as a teacher, journalist and political writer, but then began to write dictionaries and books about grammar. In 1828 he published *An American Dictionary of the English Language*, which immediately became famous.

These explanations by Mr Webster come from the 1879 edition of his standard work, which Mark Twain refers to as 'the big dictionary'.

Ăg'gra-vā'tion, *n.* [L. Lat. *aggravatio.*]
1. The act of aggravating, or making worse; — used of evils, natural or moral; the act of increasing in severity or heinousness; addition to that which is wrong. "The . . . *aggravation* of sin." *Barrow.*
2. Exaggerated representation, or heightened description of any thing wrong, improper, or unnatural. "By a little *aggravation* of the features, changed it into the Saracen's head." *Addison.*
3. Provocation; irritation. [Modern, and not legitimate.] *Dickens.*

Ăv'o-cā'tion, *n.* [Lat. *avocatio.*]
1. The act of calling aside, or diverting from some employment. "Blessed impulses to duty, and powerful *avocations* from sin." *South.*
2. The business which calls aside.
Visits, business, cards, and I know not how many other *avocations* . . . do succeed one another so thick, that in the day there is no time left for the distracted person to converse with his own thoughts. *Boyle.*
☞ The word is generally used for the smaller affairs of life, or occasional calls which summon a person to leave his ordinary or principal business. The use of this word for *vocation* is very improper.

Be-gulle' (-gīl'), *v. t.* [*imp.* & *p. p.* BEGUILED; *p. pr.* & *vb. n.* BEGUILING.] [*be* and *guile.*]
1. To delude by artifice or craft; to deceive or impose on.
The serpent *beguiled* me, and I did eat. *Gen.* iii. 13.
By expectation, every day *beguiled.* *Cowper.*
2. To elude or evade by craft.
When misery could *beguile* the tyrant's rage. *Shak.*
3. To cause to pass without notice; to amuse.
I would *beguile* the tedious day with sleep. *Shak.*
Syn. — To delude; deceive; cheat; insnare; amuse.

Căt'a-caus'tic, *a.* [Gr. κατά, against, καυστικός, burning, from καίειν, to burn; Fr. *catacaustique.*] (*Geom.* & *Optics.*) Relating to a caustic curve formed by reflection. See CAUSTIC. *Nichol.*
Căt'a-caus'tic, *n.* A caustic curve formed by reflection of light. *Nichol.*

Căt'a-chrē'sis, *n.* [Lat. *catachresis*, Gr. κατάχρησις, misuse, from καταχρῆσθαι, to misuse, from κατά, against, entirely, strengthening the sense of the simple word, and χρῆσθαι, to use.] (*Rhet.*) An abuse of a trope, or of words; a figure by which one word is wrongly put for another, or by which a word is too far wrested from its true signification; a harsh or far-fetched metaphor; as, "Her voice was but the *shadow of a sound.*" *Young.*
Căt'a-chrēs'tic, } *a.* Belonging to a catachre-
Căt'a-chrēs'tic-al, } sis; forced; far-fetched; wrested from its natural sense. "[A] *catachrestical* and improper way of speaking." *Bp. Taylor.*

Căt'a-drōme, *n.* [Gr. κατάδρομος, race-course, from κατά, down, and δρόμος, course.]
1. A race-course.
2. (*Mech.*) A machine for raising or lowering heavy weights. *Francis.*

Căt'a-dūpe, *n.* [Fr. *catadupe, catadoupe*, from Lat. *Catadupa*, Gr. Κατάδουποι, the cataracts of the Nile, from καταδουπεῖν, to fall with a loud, heavy sound, from κατά, down, and δουπεῖν, to sound heavy, δοῦπος, a dead, heavy sound.] A cataract, or waterfall. [*Obs.*] "The Egyptian *catadupes.*" *Brewer.*

Căt'al-lăc'tics, *n. sing.* [Gr. καταλλάσσειν, to exchange, from κατά, quite, and ἀλλάσσειν, to change.] The science of exchanges, or of what is now called political economy. *Whately.*

Ca-tăl'på, *n.* [From the language of the Indians of Carolina, where Catesby discovered this tree in the year 1726.] (*Bot.*) A large tree of North America, abundant on the banks of the Mississippi, having large leaves and white, showy flowers. It is the *Bignonia catalpa* of Linn., *Catalpa syringifolia* of others. *Loudon.*

Căt'a-mount, *n.* [*cat* and *mount*; Sp. *gato montes*, cat of the mountain.] (*Zoöl.*) The North American tiger; the cougar, or puma; it is the *Felis concolor* of some zoölogists, *Puma concolor* of others.

Căt'a-pĕt'al-ous, *a.* [From Gr. κατά, down, quite, against, and πεταλον, leaf.] (*Bot.*) Having the petals held together by stamens, which grow to their bases, as in the mallow. *Brande.*

Căt'a-răet, *n.* [Lat. *cataracta, cataractes*, Gr. κατ-αράκτης, καταρράκτης, from καταρρηγνύναι, to break down, pass. to fall or rush down, from κατά, down, and ῥηγνύναι, to break.]
1. A great fall of water over a precipice; a great cascade or waterfall.
The tremendous *cataracts* of America thundering in their solitudes. *W. Irving.*

Ca-tärrh' (ka-tär'), *n.* [Lat. *catarrhus*, Gr. κατάρ-ροος, contracted into κατάρρους, a running down, rheum, from καταρρεῖν, from κατά, down, and ῥεῖν, to flow.] (*Med.*) (*a.*) A discharge of fluid from the mucous membrane, especially of the nose, fauces, and bronchial passages, caused by a cold in the head. It is attended with cough, thirst, lassitude, and watery eyes. (*b.*) The cold itself.

Căt'-eall, *n.* A squeaking instrument, used in playhouses to condemn plays. *Pope.*

Căt'e-chĭsm (kăt'e-kĭzm), *n.* [Lat. *catechismus*, Gr. κατηχισμός, instruction.]
1. A form of instruction by means of questions and answers.
2. An elementary book containing a summary of principles, especially of religious doctrine, reduced to the form of questions and answers.
The Jews, even till this day, have their *catechisms.* *Hooker.*

Căt'e-gŏr'e măt'ic, *a.* [From Gr. κατηγόρημα, predicate. See CATEGORY.] (*Logic.*) Capable of being employed by itself as a term; — said of a word.

Căt'e-nāte, *v. t.* [*imp. & p. p.* CATENATED; *p. pr. & vb. n.* CATENATING.] [Lat. *catenare*, from *catena*, chain; O. H. Ger. *kétina*, *chétinna*, M. H. Ger. *kétene*, N. H. Ger. *ketten, keite*, is taken from Lat. *catena*. See CHAIN.] To connect, in a series of links or ties; to chain. [*Obs.*] *Darwin.*

Că'ter-coŭṣ'ĭn (-kŭz'n), *n.* A quater-cousin, a remote relation. See QUATER-COUSIN. *Shak.*

Căt'kin, *n.* [Diminutive of *cat*.] (*Bot.*) An ament; a species of inflorescence, consisting of many scales ranged along a slender stalk, which is the common receptacle, as in hazel, birch, oak, willow, poplar, &c.; — so called from its resemblance to a cat's tail.

Catkin of Birch.

Căt'ling, *n.* 1. A little cat. "Cat nor *catling*." *Drummond.*
2. (*Surg.*) A double-edged, sharp-pointed dismembering knife. *Harris.*

Căt'er-waul, *v. i.* [From *cat* and *waul, wawl*, to cry as a cat.] To cry as cats in rutting time; to make a harsh, offensive noise.

Căt's'-crā'dle, *n.* A familiar game played by children with a string twisted on the fingers. *Halliwell.*

Çiv'et, *n.* [Fr. *civette*, It. *zibetto*, civet and civet-cat, L. Gr. ζαπέτιον, from Per. *zabād*, civet, Ar. *zubād* and *zabbād*, the froth of milk or water, civet.]
1. A substance, of the consistence of butter or honey, taken from glands in the anal pouch of the civet (*Viverra civetta*). It is of a clear, yellowish or brownish color, of a strong, musky odor, offensive when undiluted, but agreeable when a small portion is mixed with another substance. It is used as a perfume.
2. (*Zoöl.*) The animal that produces civet (*Viverra civetta*). It is a carnivorous animal, ranking between the weasel and fox, from two to three feet long and ten or twelve inches high; of

Civet.

a brownish-gray color, with transverse black bands or spots on the body and tail. It is a native of North Africa. *Baird.*

Con-căt'e-nā'tion, *n.* [Lat. *concatenatio*.] A series of links united; a successive series or order of things connected or depending on each other.

The stoics affirmed a fatal, unchangeable *concatenation* of causes, reaching to the illicit acts of man's will. *South.*
A *concatenation* of explosions. *W. Irving.*

Con-gĕ'ri-ēṣ (-jē'rĭ-eez), *n. sing. & pl.* [Lat., from *congerere*, to bring together, from *con* and *gerere*, to bear, carry.] A collection of particles or bodies into one mass; a heap; a combination. *Berkeley.*

Cŏn'se-crate, *a.* [Lat. *consecratus*, p. p. of *consecrare*.] Consecrated; devoted; dedicated; sacred.

They were assembled in that *consecrate* place. *Bacon.*

Con-tĭg'ŭ-oŭs, *a.* [Lat. *contiguus*, from *contingere*, to touch, as it were, on all sides, from *con* and *tangere*, to touch; It. & Sp. *contiguo*, Fr. *contigu*.] In actual or close contact; touching; adjacent; near.

Joining the *contiguous* objects by the participation of their colors. *Dryden.*
Syn. — Adjoining; adjacent. See ADJOINING.

Dĕm'ī. [Fr. *demi*, from Lat. *dimidius*, half, from *di*, for *dis*, and *medius*, middle.] A prefix, signifying *half*, used in composition.
Dĕ-mī', *n.* A half-fellow at Magdalen college, Oxford. See DEMY.

De-rī'sĭve, *a.* [It. *derisivo*.] Expressing, or characterized by, derision. "*Derisive* taunts." *Pope.*

Ĕr'u-dīte, *a.* [Lat. *eruditus*, p. p. of *erudire*, to free from rudeness, to polish, to instruct, from *e*, out, from, and *rudis*, rude; Fr. *érudit*, It. & Sp. *erudito*.] Characterized by extensive reading or knowledge; well instructed; learned. "*Erudite* and metaphysical theology." *I. Taylor.*

Fra-tĕr'nal, *a.* [O. Fr., Pr., Sp., & Pg. *fraternal*, N. Fr. *fraternel*, It. *fraternale*, L. Lat. *fraternalis*, for Lat. *fraternus*, from *frater*, brother.] Pertaining to brethren; becoming brothers; brotherly; as, *fraternal* affection; a *fraternal* embrace. "*Fraternal* love and friendship." *Addison.*

A war fit for Cain to be the leader of —
An abhorred, a cursed, a *fraternal* war. *Milton.*

Gran-dĭl'o-quence, *n.* [It. *grandiloquenza*.] The use of lofty words or phrases; — usually in a bad sense; bombast.
Gran-dĭl'o-quent, *a.* [Lat. *grandis*, grand, and *loqui*, to speak.] Pompous; bombastic; grandiloquous.

Hăl'çy-on, *a.* 1. Pertaining to, or resembling, the halcyon, which was said to lay her eggs in nests on or near the sea during the calm weather about the winter solstice, which was reckoned about seven days before and as many after it.
2. Hence, calm; quiet; peaceful; undisturbed; happy. "Deep, *halcyon* repose." *De Quincey.*

Ĭm'pre-cā'tion, *n.* [Lat. *imprecatio*, Fr. *imprécation*, Sp. *imprecacion*, It. *imprecazione*.] The act of imprecating, or invoking evil on any one; a prayer that a curse or calamity may fall on any one.

Men cowered like slaves before such horrid *imprecations*. *Motley.*

Syn. — Malediction; curse; execration. See MALEDICTION.

Ĭn'can-dĕs'çent, *a.* [Lat. *incandescens*, p. pr. of *incandescere*, to become warm or hot; prefix *in* and *candescere*, to become of a glittering whiteness, to become red hot, v. incho. from *candere*, to be of a glittering whiteness; Fr. *incandescent*, Sp. & It. *incandescente*. Cf. CANDENT.] White or glowing with heat.

Holy Scripture become resplendent; or, as one might say, *incandescent* throughout. *I. Taylor.*

Mĭ'cro-scōpe, *n.* [Fr. *microscope*, It. & Sp. *microscopio*, from Gr. μικρός, small, little, and σκοπεῖν, σκέπτεσθαι, to view.] An optical instrument, consisting of a lens, or combination of lenses, for examining objects which are too minute to be viewed by the naked eye.

Microscope.

Compound microscope, an instrument consisting of one or more object lenses, usually achromatic, and an eye-piece for viewing the image formed by them, with suitable mounting for convenient use. — *Oxyhydrogen microscope* and *Solar microscope*. See OXYHYDROGEN and SOLAR. — *Single microscope*, a single convex lens used to magnify objects placed in its focus.

Mŏt'to, *n.*; *pl.* MŎT'TOĘS. [It. *motto*. See MOT.] A sentence or phrase prefixed to an essay, discourse, chapter, canto, and the like, intimating the subject of it; a brief sentence added to a device.

It was the *motto* of a bishop eminent for his piety and good works, . . . "Serve God, and be cheerful." *Addison.*

Nĕb'ū-loŭs (nĕb'yu̯-lus), *a.* [Lat. *nebulosus*, from *nebula*, q. v.; It. *nebuloso*, *nebbioso*, Sp. *nebuloso*, Fr. *nébuleux*.]
1. Cloudy; hazy. See NEBULA.
2. (*Astron.*) Pertaining to, or having the appearance of, a nebula; nebular.

Ŏs'ten-tā'tioŭs (-tā'shus), *a.* 1. Fond of excessive or offensive display; boastful.

Your modesty is so far from being *ostentatious* of the good you do. *Dryden.*

2. Evincing ostentation; pretentious. "The *ostentatious* professions of many years." *Macaulay.*
Syn. — Pompous; boastful; vaunting; showy; gaudy.

Pōle'eăt, *n.* [Either for *Polish cat*, or for *poultry-cat*, because it feeds on poultry.] (*Zoöl.*) A carnivorous mammal (*Mustela putorius*), allied to the weasel, which exhales a disagreeable odor; the fitchew or fitchet. The American polecat is often called *minx*.

Polecat (*Mustela putorius*).

Pos-tĕr'ĭ-ty, *n.* [Lat. *posteritas*, Fr. *postérité*, Pr. *posteritat*, Sp. *posteridad*, It. *posterita*. See POSTERIOR.] The race that proceeds from a progenitor; offspring to the furthest generation; the aggregate number of persons who are descended from an ancestor or a generation; — contrasted with *ancestry*.

In me all *posterity* stands cursed. *Milton.*

Prĕj'ū dĭçe, *n.* [Lat. *præjudicium*, from *præ*, before, and *judicium*, judgment; Fr. *préjudice*, It. *pregiudicio*, *pregiudizio*, Sp. *perjuicio*.]
1. Anticipative judgment; foresight. [*Obs.* and rare.] *Spenser.*
2. An opinion or decision of mind formed without due examination; prejudgment; a bias or leaning toward one side or the other of a question from other considerations than those belonging to it; an unreasonable predilection or prepossession for or against any thing; especially, an opinion or leaning adverse to any thing, formed without proper grounds, or before suitable knowledge.

Though often misled by *prejudice* and passion, he was emphatically an honest man. *Macaulay.*

3. Mischief; hurt; damage; injury.
How plain this abuse is, and what *prejudice* it does to the understanding of the sacred Scriptures! *Locke.*
He accuses me of having engaged the affections of a young lady to the *prejudice* of her pretensions. *W. Scott.*
Syn. — Prejudgment; prepossession; bias; harm; hurt; damage; detriment; mischief; disadvantage.

Re-eōurse', *n.* [Fr. *recours*, Pr. *recors*, Sp. & Pg. *recurso*, It. *ricorso*, Lat. *recursus*, from *recurrere*, *recursum*, to run back, from *re*, back, and *currere*, *cursum*, to run.]
1. Renewed course or flow; frequent passage. [*Obs.*] "Swift *recourse* of flushing blood." *Spenser.*
2. Return; renewed attack; recurrence.
Preventive physic . . . preventeth sickness in the healthy, or the *recourse* thereof in the valetudinary. *Browne.*
3. Recurrence in difficulty, perplexity, need, or the like; access or application for aid; a going for help; resort.
Thus died this great peer, in a time of great *recourse* unto him and dependence upon him. *Wotton.*
Our last *recourse* is therefore to our art. *Dryden.*
4. Access; admittance. [*Obs.*]
Give me *recourse* to him. *Shak.*

Re-eŭm'bent, *a.* [Lat. *recumbens*, p. pr. of *recumbere*. See RECUMB.]
1. Leaning; reclining; as, the *recumbent* posture of the Romans at their meals.
2. Reposing; inactive; idle. *Young.*

Sŭb-līme', *a.* [*compar.* SUBLIMER; *superl.* SUBLIMEST.] [Lat. *sublimis*, probably from *sublevare*, to lift up; Fr., It., & Sp. *sublime*. See SUBLEVATION.]
1. Lifted up; high in place; exalted aloft; — in a literal or physical sense.
Sublime on these a tower of steel is reared. *Dryden.*
2. Distinguished by lofty or noble traits; eminent; — said of persons.
The age was fruitful in great men, but if we except the *sublime* Julian leader, none, as regards splendor of endowments, stood upon the same level as Cicero. *De Quincey.*

3. Awakening or expressing the emotion of awe, adoration, veneration, heroic resolve, and the like; dignified; grand; solemn; stately; — said of an impressive object in nature, of a noble action, of a discourse, of a work of art, of a spectacle, and the like; as, *sublime* scenery; a *sublime* deed.

> Easy in style thy work, in sense *sublime*. *Prior.*

4. Elevated by joy; elate; as, *sublime* with expectation.

> Their hearts were jocund and *sublime*,
> Drunk with idolatry, drunk with wine. *Milton.*

5. Lofty of mien; elevated in manner. [*Rare.*]

> His fair, large front, and eye *sublime* declared
> Absolute rule. *Milton.*

Syn. — Grand; exalted; lofty; noble; majestic. See GRAND.

Sü′per-fï′cial (-fĭsh′al), *a.* [Lat. *superficialis*, Fr. *superficiel*, Pr., Sp., & Pg. *superficial*, It. *superficiale*. See SUPERFICIES.]

1. Lying on, or pertaining to, the superficies or surface; shallow; not deep; as, a *superficial* color; a *superficial* covering; *superficial* measure or contents.

2. Reaching or comprehending only what is obvious or apparent; not deep or profound; shallow; as, a *superficial* scholar; *superficial* knowledge; — said especially in respect to study, learning, and the like.

Sȳn′o-nȳm, *n.*: *pl.* SȲN′O-NȲMṢ. [Written also *synonyme*.] [Fr. *synonyme*, Gr. συνώνυμον. See SYNONYMOUS.] One of two or more words in the same language which are the precise equivalents of each other, or which have very nearly the same signification, and therefore are liable to be confounded together.

> All languages tend to clear themselves of *synonyms* as intellectual culture advances, the superfluous words being taken up and appropriated by new shades and combinations of thought evolved in the progress of society. *De Quincey.*

> Few languages are richer than English in approximate *synonyms* and conjugates. *G. P. Marsh.*

> His name has thus become, throughout all civilized countries, a *synonym* for probity and philanthropy. *Macaulay.*

Tĕn′dril, *n.* [Fr. *tendron*, *tendrillon*, from *tendre*, Eng. *tender*, properly the tender branch or sprig of a plant. Cf. It. *tenerume*, id., from *tenero*, tender.] (*Bot.*) A filiform, spiral shoot of a plant that winds round another body for the purpose of support.

Tĕn′dril, *a.* Clasping; climbing as a tendril.

Thrīçe, *adv.* [O. Eng. *thries*, from *three*, with the termination of a genitive; A-S. *thriga*, *thriwa*.]

1. Three times.

> Before the cock crow, thou shalt deny me *thrice*. *Matt.* xxvi. 34.

> *Thrice* is he armed that hath his quarrel just. *Shak.*

2. Repeatedly; earnestly; emphatically; very.

> *Thrice* noble lord, let me entreat of you
> To pardon me. *Shak.*

Tôr′pid, *a.* [Lat. *torpidus*, from *torpere*, to be stiff, numb, or torpid; Fr. *torpide*, It. *torpido*, Sp. *torpe*.]

1. Having lost motion, or the power of exertion and feeling; numb; as, a *torpid* limb.

> Without heat all things would be *torpid*. *Ray.*

2. Dull; stupid; sluggish; inactive.

Syn. — Dull; stupid; sluggish; inactive; benumbed.

Trụ′eu-lent (110), *a.* [Lat. *truculentus*, from *trux, trucis*, wild, fierce; O. Fr. *truculent*, Sp. & It. *truculento*.]

1. Fierce; savage; barbarous; as, the *truculent* inhabitants of Scythia. *Ray.*

2. Of ferocious aspect. *Johnson.*

3. Cruel; destructive; ruthless. "More or less *truculent* plagues." *Harvey.*

Trụ′eu-lent-ly, *adv.* In a truculent manner; fiercely; destructively.

Vĭ-çĭs′sĭ-tūde (53), *n.* [Fr. *vicissitude*, Sp. *vicisitud*, Pg. *vicissitude*, It. *vicissitudine*, Lat. *vicissitudo*, from *vicis*, change, turn.]

1. Regular change or succession from one thing to another; alternation; mutual succession; interchange.

> God made two great lights . . .
> To illuminate the earth and rule the day
> In their *vicissitude*, and rule the night. *Milton.*

2. Change; revolution; mutation, as in human affairs.

> This man had, after many *vicissitudes* of fortune, sunk at last into abject poverty. *Macaulay.*

Wĕl′kin, *n.* [A-S. *wolcen*, *welcn*, cloud, air, sky, heaven, O. Sax. *wolcan*, O. Fries. *wolken*, *ulken*, O. H. Ger. *wolchan*, M. H. Ger. *wolken*, N. H. Ger. *wolke*, L. Ger. *wulke*, Skr. *valâhaka*, a cloud.] The visible regions of the air; the vault of heaven; the sky. "The fair *welkin* foully overcast." *Spenser.* "When storms the *welkin* rend." *Wordsworth.*